IMPRESSIONS of the

BRECON
BEACONS

Produced by AA Publishing
© AA Media Limited 2009

Published by AA Publishing (a trading name of AA Media Limited,
whose registered office is Fanum House, Basing View, Basingstoke, Hampshire
RG21 4EA; registered number 06112600)

ISBN: 978-0-7495-6409-4

A04066

A CIP catalogue record for this book is available from the British Library.

The contents of this book are believed correct at the time of printing. Nevertheless,
the publishers cannot be held responsible for any errors, omissions or for changes in
the details given in this book or for the consequences of any reliance on the
information provided by the same. This does not affect your statutory rights.

Printed and bound in China by C & C Offset Printing Co. Ltd

Opposite: The distinctive outline of the magnificent Black Mountains at sunset.

IMPRESSIONS of the

BRECON
BEACONS

Picture Acknowledgements

The Automobile Association would like to thank the following photographers, companies and picture libraries for their assistance in the preparation of this book.

Abbreviations for the picture credits are as follows: (t) top; (b) bottom; (l) left; (r) right; (AA) AA World Travel Library.

Front Cover AA/D Santillo; Back Cover (main) AA/D Santillo; Back Cover (inset) AA/C Molyneux; 3 AA/D Santillo; 5 AA/D Santillo; 7 AA/I Burgum; 10 AA/C Molyneux; 11 AA/C&A Molyneux; 12 AA/C&A Molyneux; 13 AA/I Burgum; 14 AA/I Burgum; 15 ffotoCymru – Images of Wales/Alamy; 16 AA/C Nicholls; 17 Graham Morley/Alamy; 18 AA; 19 Simon Tilley Commercial/Alamy; 20 Rod McLean/Alamy; 21 Oliver Smart/Alamy; 22 James Osmond Photography/Alamy; 23 AA/D Santillo; 24 David Noble Photography/Alamy; 25 Jeff Morgan tourism and leisure/Alamy; 26 AA/I Burgum; 27 The Photolibrary Wales/Alamy; 28 AA/C Molyneux; 29 Nic Cleave Photography/Alamy; 30 The Photolibrary Wales/Alamy; 31 AA/D Santillo; 32 Simon Tilley/Alamy; 33 AA/D Santillo; 34 Matt Botwood/Alamy; 35 AA/D Santillo; 36 Ben Pipe/ Alamy; 37 AA/I Burgum; 38 AA/N Jenkins; 39 Robin Weaver/Alamy; 40 AA/D Santillo; 41 Allen Lloyd/Alamy; 42 The Photolibrary Wales/Alamy; 43 Simon Tilley Commercial/Alamy; 44 AA/N Jenkins; 45 AA/D Santillo; 46 AA/N Jenkins; 47 Matt Botwood (C Stock)/Alamy; 48 David Norton Photography/Alamy; 49 AA/D Santillo; 50 AA/D Santillo; 51 Stephen Peter Street/Alamy; 52 Peter Rhoades/Alamy; 53 The National Trust Photolibrary/Alamy; 54 David Rose/Alamy; 55 AA/N Jenkins; 56 AA/D Santillo; 57 Rod McLean/Alamy; 58 Graham Bell/Alamy; 59 Robert Read/Alamy; 60 The Photolibrary Wales/Alamy; 61 David Angel/Alamy; 62 Gordon Scammell/Alamy; 63 The Photolibrary Wales/Alamy; 64 AA/D Santillo; 65 Mark Salter/Alamy; 66 AA/D Santillo; 67 The Photolibrary Wales/Alamy; 68 The Photolibrary Wales/Alamy; 69 The Photolibrary Wales/Alamy; 70 Robert Read/Alamy; 71 The Photolibrary Wales/Alamy; 72 Nick Turner/Alamy; 73 AA/D Santillo; 74 AA/C&A Molyneux; 75 Robert Read/Alamy; 76 AA/D Santillo; 77 Joan Gravell/Alamy; 78 The Photolibrary Wales/Alamy; 79 Chris Howes/Wild Places Photography/Alamy; 80 AA/D Santillo; 81 Nick Turner/Alamy; 82 AA/D Santillo; 83 AA/D Santillo; 84 AA/D Santillo; 85 Simon Tilley/Alamy; 86 Nick Turner/Alamy; 87 Philip Veale/Alamy; 88 The Photolibrary Wales/Alamy; 89 David Norton Photography/Alamy; 90 Craig Joiner Photography/Alamy; 91 AA/D Santillo; 92 The National Trust Photolibrary/Alamy; 93 AA/D Santillo; 94 AA/C&A Molyneux; 95 AA/I Burgum.

Every effort has been made to trace the copyright holders, and we apologise in advance for any accidental errors. We would be happy to apply the corrections in the following edition of this publication.

Opposite: Offa's Dyke National Trail at the summit of Hay Bluff near Hay-on-Wye.

INTRODUCTION

The Brecon Beacons National Park is very much the 'home range' of the 'townies', who visit the park in search of escape, adventure, breathtaking scenery and, perhaps, some respite from the grind of urban life. Designated a National Park in 1957, the Brecon Beacons stretches from Llandeilo in the west to Abergavenny in the east, and between Llandovery and Hay-on-Wye on the northern boundary and the heads of the industrial valleys that define the southern perimeters. The National Park covers a total area of 519 square miles (1,344sq km) and the western half of the park, Forest Fawr, was awarded European and Global Geopark status in 2005 for its geological heritage.

The Brecon Beacons National Park consists of four great mountain ranges – the Black Mountains in the east, the Brecon Beacons, Fforest Fawr, and the Black Mountain in the west, which form the spine of the park. Many of the sandstone escarpments have finely sculpted north faces and table-like summits. The Brecon Beacons valleys are fertile, green and lush, but to the north the scenery transforms into the wild remote hills of mid-Wales.

In addition, there are a few superb outliers in the National Park, such as the Blorenge, which dominates the small finger of the park that points southwards from Abergavenny to Pontypool and overlooks the UNESCO World Heritage site of Blaenavon – an exceptional example of industrial South Wales. Another unmissable sight is Ysgyryd Fawr or Skirrid Mountain, often referred to as Holy Mountain. The evangelical importance of the mountain is marked with the remains of a small medieval place of worship, dedicated to St Michael, which is squeezed on to the narrow summit. And lastly, the Sugar Loaf, with its distinctive dome that dominates the Abergavenny skyline.

The big attraction of the park, however, is the mountain ranges. In the east the Black Mountains push up against the English border. Around Capel-y-ffin and the Vale of Ewyas, finger-like ridges of mountains divide steep sided valleys spreading down to the towns of Abergavenny and Crickhowell. Craig y Fan Ddu, Waun Fach and Y Grib offer airy ridges with far-reaching views, west to the Brecons and east over England.

It is the central peaks, or the true 'Brecon Beacons', that see the most adulation. As well as boasting the highest ground in Southern Britain, their tabletop summits preside over some of the finest upland scenery in Britain and the high, whale-backed sweeps of sandstone that gave their name to the National Park. The loftiest, Pen y Fan, is the highest mountain in southern Britain, and also one of the most accessible, but there are other summits. Corn Du, Cribyn and Fan Fryncych are all shapely eminences with plenty of upland. The latter has its soul in the rugged landscape known as the Fforest Fawr, part of the 300-square-mile (762sq km) Geopark, which includes mountains, moorlands and wooded valleys. At its feet, the limestone has fissured and cracked into myriad caves and waterfalls, best seen in the woodlands near Ystradfellte, which is also known as Waterfall Country. The landscape here is completely different to that of the remote, windswept escarpments, but the wooded gorges and stunning waterfalls are equally marvellous.

The last area of the national park is also the remotest. The Black Mountain rises above the Towy Valley to the west and guards the source of the River Usk. The ridge of Bannau Sir Gaer, better known as Carmarthen Fan offers a glimpse of truly wild landscape and perhaps a sighting of a Red Kite.

Opposite: The highlight of the Waterfall Country is Sgwd y Eira, where it is possible to venture behind the falls to admire the cascade of water.

Dusk over the forested shores of the Usk Reservoir, which is famous for its salmon and trout fishing and popular with walkers and cyclists.
Opposite: In the distance, the wild and remote Black Mountain range rises above the lush, rolling hills of the Towy Valley.

The Black Mountains are a hill-walkers paradise; deep cloven valleys and the lumbering, whaleback ridges of Craig y Fan Ddu, Waun Fach and Y Grib, which are literally riddled with tracks and trails to explore.

The grand sweeping architecture of Taf Fechan Valley and the grassy shores of the Lower Neuadd Reservoir, opened in 1884 to provide water for Merthyr Tydfil, nestling within the uplands. In the background, the unmistakable outline of Pen y Fan.

Sunset over the Usk Reservoir. Located in the uplands and with tremendous views of Carmathan Fan, the reservoir and woodland supports the Marsh Fritillary butterfly, the Red Kite, as well as common woodland birds and wildfowl. Opposite: The spectacular falls of Sgwd y Pannwr located in the dense woodland of the Vale of Neath, Ystradfellte.

Looking across the Tarell Valley to the true kings of the park, Pen y Fan and Corn Du, whose lofty crowns command attention. The National Trust owns more than 9,000 acres (3,645ha) in the Brecon Beacons National Park including Pen y Fan and Corn Du.

The might and stature of Pen y Fan is clear from almost any viewpoint, but the views from the top are magnificent as the northeast face falls precipitously down more than 1,000 feet (305m) to the rolling moorland of Cwm Sere below.

The rolling green hills of Radnorshire to the north of Hay-on-Wye. Set by the banks of the River Wye and sheltered by the Black Mountains, the historic town of Hay-on-Wye marks both the northernmost point of the National Park and the Anglo-Welsh border.

The southern flank of Pwll Du is characterised by heather and tussock moorland, which is inhabited by red grouse, while the northern flanks boast a Bronze-Age burial cairn and the ground above the escarpment is littered with grass-covered mounds, a remnant of past quarrying.

The sheep that graze the upland commons in the National Park are mainly the hardy Welsh mountain sheep. The smallest of the commercially bred sheep, Welsh mountain sheep typically have a small head, small ears and a white or tanned face with dark eyes.

Believed to be descended from Celtic stock, Welsh mountain ponies have roamed the mountains for more than a 1000 years, despite being threatened with extinction over the centuries. Today, the ponies are prized for their resilient natures.

The remote nature of the Black Mountain links this area, more than any other, with one of Britain's most beautiful birds, the Red Kite.
Opposite: Early morning mist over the stunning deciduous woodland, which forms a rich and valuable habitat for wildlife.

Looking towards Cribyn, in the Brecon Beacons range, at sunrise. At an elevation of 2,608 feet (795m) Cribyn's summit lies on a ridge up from the wooded slopes of the Talybont Reservoir and connects to Pen y Fan by a ridge to the west and Fan y Big in the east.

Cairn on the summit of Garreg Lwyd, also known as Moel Gornach – a subsidiary summit of Fan Brycheiniog – at an elevation of 2,021 feet (616m). The majority the Black Mountain range is made up of barren, windswept moorland, which is home to the Red Kite and possesses an austere beauty. Unusually, a large percentage of the land is actually owned by the National Park Authority.

To the east of the National Park, lies the Black Mountains – Craig y Fan Ddu, Waun Fach and Y Grib. The steep western slopes of the towering massif are accentuated by a succession of grassy arêtes and rounded promontories which hide a multitude of remote and picturesque cwms.

Wooden footbridge across the Afon Pyrddin, Pontneddfechan, in Waterfall Country. While the woods that line the banks of the rivers are home to many species of birds, the river itself is likely to give sightings of two fairly distinctive species – the dipper, usually seen bobbing up and down on rocks in mid-stream, and the grey wagtail.

Sheep on the snow-lined slopes of the peaceful valley of Cwm Oergwm. The hardy animals thrive in the harsh mountain environment – the ewes spend as many as 36 weeks each year on high ground – and are adept at making the best out of the very poor grazing available.

The falls of Sgwd Gwladus, meaning 'Waterfall of the Chieftain', in Pontneddfechan. The falls are the result of a geological fault that pushed the sandstone against softer shales and the eroding force of the rivers, which has left shelves of the harder rock exposed.

Gospel Pass, a glacier-shaped valley, which is believed to be one of the routes used by early religious settlers and farmers from the north.
Opposite: The barren, windswept moorland of the Black Mountain Range with a magnificent view to the steepest section
of Carmarthen Fan, which is also known as Bannau Sir Gaer.

Every mountain has its 'trade route' – the easiest and most trafficked way to the top – and Pen y Fan is no different. The most commonly used tactic is an out-and-back approach, using an eroded footpath ascending to Pen y Fan.

Mushrooms growing on Offa's Dyke Path, near Hay-on-Wye. In an attempt to keep the Welsh to the west, King Offa, the 8th-century ruler of Mercia, decided to mark out his borders using a ditch and an earth wall to strengthen any natural boundaries such as rivers or ridges. It ran from Prestatyn to Chepstow, at the mouth of the River Wye and, in places, it was more than 20 feet (6m) high and 60 feet (18m) wide.

*A telephone kiosk near the Storey Arms Centre, which marks the beginning of a linear walk along a section of the Taff Trail
— the line of the old road that ran between Merthyr Tydfil and Brecon. In those days the Storey Arms was a coaching inn.*

Looking down over the wooded Talybont Forest towards the magnificent 2-mile (3km) long Talybont Reservoir.
The diverse landscape – from upland and moorland to forest and open water – provides rich habitats for badgers,
otters, polecats, hares, foxes and bats as well as wildfowl, waders and raptors.

The National Park Authority provides consultation to landowners wishing to keep the more scenic traditional crafts, such as dry stone walls, alive, although many of the hedgerows and walls that once divided the land are expensive to maintain and have been replaced by wire fences.

View over the barren and windswept moorland of the Black Mountain, Y Mynydd Du, to the brooding black waters of Llyn y Fan Fawr − one of two glacial lakes on the summit of Fan Brycheiniog.

The bracken covered hillside below the summit of Waun Rydd in southern Powys reaches a height of 2,523 feet (769m).

Opposite: The fertile valleys of the Brecon Beacons, with fields as green and lush as those of Ireland, are a haven of tranquillity.

Superb riverside scenery of the River Neath, Afon Nedd in Welsh, in spate near the Ystradfellte waterfalls on the southern fringes of the park.

The Sugar Loaf, or Mynydd Pen-y-fal to give it its Welsh name, and some of the land that surrounds it, belongs to the National Trust, who own around 4 per cent of the land within the National Park. The distinctive, cone-shaped outline of its rock-strewn summit is visible for miles around.

Carreg Cennen Castle occupies an airy perch atop precipitous limestone cliffs and commands fine views in all directions.
Opposite: Pen y Fan, the highest peak in southern Britain, viewed from Mynydd Iltyd Common near the Mountain Centre.

The banks of the Waterfall Country, just south of the tiny village of Ystradfellte, are particularly beautiful in September and October, when the magnificent beech woods show off a full spectrum of autumn colours.

The Welsh mountain pony, although classed as a rare breed, is a familiar sight all over the Brecon Beacons. The ponies graze all year-round and are important in keeping the uplands of the National Park in good condition.

The spectacular summits of Pen y Fan, Corn Du and Cribyn were once all crowned with Bronze Age burial cairns, probably dating back to around 1800 BC. It's clear that the mountains held some significance, even at that time.

Summit cairn and shelter on Moel Gornach, in the Black Mountain range. A layer of carboniferous limestone overlies the old red sandstone and this younger rock is soluble in the slightly acidic rain. The result is huge tracts of moorland peppered with sinkholes and caves.

Llangorse Lake is well known for its ecology, particularly birdlife, which is protected by a nature reserve on the southern shores. The water attracts a huge number of wintering birds, as well as acting as a stop-off for species that migrate.

Maen Llia takes on mystical qualities at sunset. This massive monolith lies at the junction of two valleys, a short distance from Ystradfellte. Its original purpose is unknown although it is possible that it served as an ancient territorial marker or trackway.

The snow-capped whaleback ridge of Cribyn from Pen y Fan in winter. Looking north from Pen y Fan, Brecon can be spied, tucked away at the foot of the mountains. It's the largest town in the National Park and also the administrative centre of the park authority.

Hay-on-Wye Castle has a woeful history. Built in the 13th century by William de Breos, the baron soon fell out with King John and fled to France, leaving his castle to be sacked and his wife and children to starve to death. Further attacks and fire has left the castle in ruins.

Offa's Dyke National Trail, opened in 1971, follows a similar line to King Offa's original 8th-century earthworks.
Opposite: Dawn breaks in the National Park, and this is the best time for spotting skylarks and meadow pipits,
both are small, mottled brown birds and a familiar sight on the grassy slopes of the uplands.

South of the upland plateaux of Fforest Fawr, geological faults and water erosion have produced a series of deep, narrow gorges, sheltered by woodland and randomly broken up by gushing waterfalls. This pocket of dramatic limestone scenery is often referred to as Waterfall Country.

An autumn view of the spectacular Glyn Tarell, which supports a range of unique habitats. The deep hollow was formed by the action of an ice-age glacier, and the retreating ice left a legacy of arctic-alpine plants that were sheltered from rising temperatures by the north-facing escarpment.

Nestling beneath the delightful Mynydd Llangorse and overlooked by the even shaplier Mynydd Troeg, is Llangorse Lake – the largest natural lake in South Wales. This shallow, glacier-scoured expanse of water is popular with walkers and birders.

Steep and rocky ground leads from the table-top summit of Pen y Fan, with the grassy flanks of Cribyn, appearing to be much steeper than actually are, ahead. Far below the summits lie the beautiful ice-sculpted cwms of Llwch, Sere, Cynwyn and Oergwm.

Vista across the Talybont Reservoir to the Black Mountains in the distance. The open water forms an important site for wildfowl and raptors, and there is a hide overlooking a protected wetland area at the southern end of the reservoir.

Mist over the Brecon Beacons National Park at dawn.

Located on the eastern end of the impressive Black Mountains escarpment, the steep slopes of Hay Bluff with views over the Wye Valley.
Opposite: The spectacular view across Fforest Fawr from the huge cairn on top of Corn Du's broad summit plateau.

The might and stature Corn Du and Pen y Fan is clear from any viewpoint – the sheer scale of the drop from the north face of Corn Du and the incomparable north east face of Pen y Fan, which falls precipitously down over 1,000 feet (305m) to the rolling moorland of Cwm Sere below.

Far Fawr, the highest and easiest to access mountain in this area of the park, is usually refreshingly free of crowds as the untracked moorland of Fforest Fawr sees far fewer visitors than other mountains in the National Park.

A Welsh mountain sheep on the side of a valley with the Sugar Loaf, one the most popular mountains in the National Park, in the distance. The distinctive, cone-shaped outline of the rock-strewn summit is visible from miles around.

The National Trust cares for more than 9,000 acres (3,645ha) of the Brecon Beacons National Park, including the highest summit at Pen y Fan and the dramatic outlier of Ysgyryd Fawr. The Trust was founded in 1895 with the objective of protecting places of beauty and value from the onslaught of industrial development – particularly pertinent in South Wales.

Inside a book shop in Hay-on-Wye, a vibrant market town famous for its 30-plus secondhand and antiquarian bookshops. Among the town's maze of narrow streets there are also many fascinating old buildings, including a colonnaded 19th-century butter market, and the 16th-century Three Tuns pub.

View from behind the spectacular Henrhyd Falls, near Coelbren, a 90-foot (27m) cascade of water from Farewell Rock into a beautiful wooded gorge. This is the highest waterfall in the Fforest Fawr Geopark.

The Monmouthshire and Brecon Canal, built between 1797 and 1812, represents a remarkable feat of engineering, given the mountainous terrain that it traverses, with more than 23 miles (37km) of its total 33 miles (53km) being level.

The deciduous trees, mainly consisting of oak, birch and ash, along towpath of the Monmouthshire and Brecon Canal provide an important habitat for small birds, especially those of the garden variety, including most members of the tit family, robins and wrens.

Wales has one of the highest densities of sheep in the world. In the Brecon Beacons National Park they outnumber people by 30 to 1.
Most of the farms in the National Park are sheep farms, but many also maintain small herds of beef cattle on the lower ground.

A blaze of autumn colour on Heather Mynydd Illtyd Common, named after St Illtyd, a Welsh-born monk who founded the nearby abbey of Llan-Illtut. He is perhaps most famous for his fights against famine, which included sailing grain ships to Brittany in the early 6th century.

Ysgyryd Fawr has long been referred to as the Holy Mountain. The deep cleft in the ridge is said to have been created by a freak bolt of lightning at the time of the crucifixion and the soil in the valley that divides the hillsides is thought to have special powers.

Welsh mountain pony grazing at Twmpa, often referred to as 'Lord Hereford's Knob in the Black Mountains.

View towards Corn Du from Pen y Fan, the summit rocks of Corn Du overhang the chasm below.

View over the sandstone massif of Fforest Fawr and the Black Mountain, which is comprised of a series of fans (or hills) with Fan Fawr at the highest point and two glacial lakes of Llyn y Fan Fach and Llyn y Fan Fawr.

The trail of the western side of the River Usk with the Black Mountain in the distance. It is the longest river in the Fforest Fawr Geopark and is designated an SSSI (Site of Special Scientific Interest) because of its various fish species and otter population.

View over the Wye Valley from a rock outcrop along Hay Bluff in the Brecon Beacons.

Offa's Dyke National Trail opened in 1971 and follows the north–south line of the dyke for 177 miles (285km) and showcases the incredible diversity of the Welsh countryside.

A windblown hawthorn tree lies in deep snow in the Black Mountain.

Ash and oak trees predominate in the park, which together with the under-canopy of hazel and hawthorn, form a rich wildlife habitat.
Opposite: Walker admiring the view from the summit of Pen y Fan at sunset.

Hay-on-Wye is a bustling, colourful settlement with an upbeat atmosphere, which is totally different from the local farming communities, and tourists come from all over the world to visit the annual literary festival.

The landscape of the Brecon Beacons has long been dominated by farming but the principle aim of the National Park Authorities is to balance the needs of the landscape and the environment with the demands of visitors and the well-being of local communities, a tightrope that it manages very effectively.

Carreg Cennen is fairly unique for a Welsh castle in that it was built by the Welsh rather than the Normans. The current layout of the castle was constructed in the 12th century, although a Roman coin found on the site is evidence of earlier settlement.

Looking down the huge, grassy slopes of the Vale of Ewyas, which displays the classic U-shape of its ice-age roots, in the direction of Capel-y-ffin in the Black Mountains.

In the Valley of Usk, between Brecon and Abergavenny, is the impressive Norman-built edifice of Tretower,
a superb motte-and-bailey castle with a restored medieval house and garden.

Walking through Llangasty Nature Reserve on the southern shores of Llangorse Lake. The lake is well known for its ecology, particularly birdlife. Another important inhabitant is the Small Bluetail dragonfly, Ischnura pumilio, *which is thought to breed only in one other spot in Britain.*

With more than 620 miles (1000km) of public rights of way and a huge variety of upland areas to choose from, it is not surprising that horse-riding, walking and climbing are the most popular activities in the park.

Aside from its natural charms, the most notable feature of Llangorse Lake is its crannog, or artificial island.
Its access causeway has long since disappeared and today it lies roughly 44yds (40m) from the shore.

Swathes of colourful foxgloves and farmland near Talybont on Usk.

Opposite: Craig Cerrig-gleisiad is a true spectacle, and a unique environment, which hosts a range of habitats that supports a number of rare species of flora and fauna. The lower slopes are home to mixed woodland and flowers, while the high ground supports heather and bilberry, 16 species of butterfly have been recorded and more than 80 different types of birds, including the ring ouzel and the peregrine falcon.

Towering above the mountain hub of Crickhowell, Table Mountain appears as a flat-topped knoll tucked beneath the screes of Pen Cerrig-calch.
It is topped by the ramparts of an impressive Iron-Age fort known as Crug Hywel, which translates to 'Hywel's Fort.'

Looking down onto Talybont Reservoir, which was built in the 1930s to supply water to Newport. It is the largest reservoir of still water in the Brecon Beaons National Park and has many fishing, cycling and walking opportunities.

Pen y Fan in the distance. This is the highest peak in southern Britain and the closest real mountain to a huge chunk of the population, attracting mass pilgrimages from the London, the Home Counties, Birmingham, Bristol and South Wales.

The hardy Welsh mountain sheep thrive in the harsh mountain environment – the ewes spend as many as 36 weeks every year on the high ground – and are adept at eking a living out of the very poor grazing available.

Surrounded by myths and legends, Maen Llia has stood in grand isolation for more than a thousand years.
Opposite: At the foot of Pen y Fan, Cwm Llwch is a fine example of a mountain lake left behind by the last ice age.

INDEX